9/05

BT

8/2012

Mysterious Encounters

Ghost Ships

by Kevin Hile

KIDHAVEN PRESS
A part of Gale, Cengage Learning

GALE
CENGAGE Learning™

Detroit • New York • San Francisco • New Haven, Conn • Waterville, Maine • London

LIBRARY OF CONGRESS CATALOGING-IN-PUBLICATION DATA

Hile, Kevin.
    Ghost ships / by Kevin Hile.
        p. cm. — (Mysterious encounters)
    Includes bibliographical references and index.
    ISBN 978-0-7377-4086-8 (hardcover)
    1. Ghosts—Juvenile literature. 2. Apparitions—Juvenile literature. 3.
Shipwrecks—Miscellanea—Juvenile literature. I. Title.
    BF1486.H55 2009
    133.1'22—dc22
                                                            2008029078

KidHaven Press
27500 Drake Rd.
Farmington Hills, MI 48331

ISBN-13: 978-0-7377-4086-8
ISBN-10: 0-7377-4086-8

Printed in the United States of America
1 2 3 4 5 6 7 12 11 10 09 08

Contents

Chapter 1

Hazy Origins of the Ghost Ship

In the popular 2006 movie *Pirates of the Caribbean: Dead Man's Chest*, Captain Jack Sparrow (played by Johnny Depp) is pursued by the evil Davy Jones, captain of the *Flying Dutchman*. Captain Sparrow, it seems, is marked for death by Jones, the squid-faced ruler of the evil powers of the sea.

As Hollywood often does, the writers and directors mangle the original tales to fit the purposes of the movie. In this case the character of Jones and his story are a mix of several **myths** and **legends** of the sea that go back for centuries. The movie combines three fearful stories into one. There is Davy Jones, the spirit who takes sailors to their deaths and places them in his undersea locker. Then there are sea monsters, as seen in Jones's appearance in the movie. In the original stories he is completely human in appearance. Lastly the movie uses the legend of ghost ships—specifically the legend of the *Flying Dutchman*.

On this last point, the movie writers make a common mistake. The "Flying Dutchman" is the nickname of a sea captain, not a ship, which has no name in the myths.

Fact and fiction can be tricky definitions. It is hard to blame a Hollywood studio for mixing up a story about ghosts and cursed crews that are not actually based on true events in history. Yet there are many people who believe the tales of ghost ships, even to this day. How such stories get started is a complicated tale in itself.

The tentacle-faced Davy Jones, captain of the *Flying Dutchman*, is the villain of the 2006 Disney movie *Pirates of the Caribbean: Dead Man's Chest*, which includes parts of several age-old myths and legends of the sea in its plot.

Dangers of the Sea

Ghost ships and other scary stories about the ocean have their origins in common human fears. When some people think of an ocean trip, what comes to their minds might be a pleasant voyage on a cruise ship or perhaps sailing on a **yacht** on a lake. The sea, however, has always been a dangerous place for humans, full of violent storms, hidden rocky **shoals** that smash ship **hulls**, bloodthirsty pirates, and other perils.

Even today being on a sailing **vessel** can be risky. In a popular television program called *Deadliest Catch: Crab Fishing in Alaska*, the risks sailors take today to make a living is very apparent. Massive

Crewmen aboard modern-day fishing vessels and other oceangoing ships face dangers from storms and rough seas similar to those experienced by sailors throughout history.

The Kraken

Perhaps the most terrifying sea monster legend of all concerns the kraken. The kraken was a giant squid strong enough to pull entire ships below the waves. Interestingly, it is based on fact. There exist real-life, deep-sea squid large enough to fight whales.

The legendary sea monster known as the kraken is depicted attacking a ship while sailors flee in terror.

ocean waves can easily sink a boat, and fishers are routinely injured on the rocking vessel, often by their own equipment. Almost 3,000 people working aboard ships die each year at sea.[1]

Before sailors had sophisticated navigational systems, radio communications, and weather satellites, the sea was a mysterious place. Before the 19th century, many of the world's continents and islands remained unknown. When ships disappeared, never to be heard from again, stories were invented to explain the tragedies. In fact, before explorers such as Ferdinand Magellan traveled around the world by ship in the early 16th century, most people believed ships could fall off the edge of the world or be eaten by sea serpents if they traveled too far.

Sailor Superstitions

Though it is less true today, perhaps, than in the past, sailors are known for being superstitious. **Superstitions** originate from the belief that certain things—no matter how silly they might seem—cause other things to happen. For example, sailors used to believe that throwing a shoe at a ship brought good luck. On the other hand, to point a finger at a ship was bad luck, but it was all right if you used your entire hand to gesture at a ship.

Other superstitions told sailors the best time to sail out of port, which sea life to avoid, and even how to decorate a ship. The reason old sailing vessels used to have wood carvings of a woman on the prow of the ship was that sailors believed this would keep storms away.

Some superstitions had some basis in common sense, though. For instance, there was a natural dread of keeping a dead body aboard a ship, since there was a very real threat that the corpse could

Wood carvings of women, like this one that was once mounted on the prow of an 18th-century ship, were often used to decorate ships because superstitious sailors believed they would keep storms away.

spread disease to the other sailors. Some of the practices associated with a death were less logical, though, such as putting the corpse into a hammock and sewing it closed with thirteen stitches. The body was then nailed into a coffin to make sure the ghost could not get out.

Omens of Death

The fear of death is a common theme among most of these superstitions. Sailors often interpreted natural **phenomena** as **omens** that they were heading for danger or possibly death. One such weather-related sight is known as **Saint Elmo's fire**. This is a real phenomenon that occurs in electrical storms. The electricity in the air can make parts of a ship light up. Sailors saw this as a good or bad omen, depending on what section of the ship was illuminated: "Sailors believed its appearance was a sign that the worst of the storm was over," said author Cindy Vallar on her Web site, "and as long as the

Sailors once connected the appearance of Saint Elmo's fire, a natural phenomenon that makes parts of a ship glow because of electricity in the air, with the fate of their voyage.

light remained high among the **masts**, luck followed them. If it shone on the deck, though, bad luck was certain. If the light ringed a man's head, he would soon die."[2]

This connection between the glow of lightning on a ship's deck or around a person's head and the superstition of death may explain why many ghost ships are associated with an eerie glow, too.

While death sometimes came from natural events such as storms, at other times, sailors believed that death actively pursued them. Sharks or manta rays seen swimming near a ship were a bad omen.

Similarly, seeing a ghost ship was often considered a bad omen that meant the person would soon die. This was particularly true of the legend of the *Flying Dutchman*, though other ghost ships also brought with them similar omens of death.

Fact or Fiction?

Not all sightings of ghost ships are reported by sailors. Sometimes people spot these vessels from the shore, and these tales often become local **folklore**. What makes any myth or legend interesting and appealing is that one can find a kernel of truth in almost any such tale. In the case of ghost ships, there are some stories that are almost definitely complete fiction. In fact, the popularity of such

Optical Illusions

One possible scientific explanation of ghost ships involves an optical illusion caused by light. The image of a ship beyond the horizon could, in theory, reflect off clouds and appear as a ghostly ship.

tales as the *Flying Dutchman* owes much to fiction writers and artists referring to it in their work. The *Flying Dutchman* appeared in works from authors such as Washington Irving and Sir Arthur Conan Doyle and in works of the German opera composer Richard Wagner.

Other tales of mysterious ships—especially those from modern sources—seem to have much more fact to them. Indeed, a few modern mysteries have been resolved after some investigation.

Depending on whether or not there are eyewitnesses, a story about a ghost ship can be easier or more difficult to disprove. Clearly, when a story is passed down as part of folklore, it is easier to believe that it is just a story. Other times witnesses to an event will swear that they saw a ghost ship.

Explanations for such accounts are varied. Sometimes it might be psychological—for example, a widow of a sailor wishing to see her lost husband's ship might think she sees the vessel. Many tales of ghost ships involve fog or storms or other types of weather that might reasonably make shadows or rocks appear to be ships.

There are tales, too, that are more difficult to explain away.

Chapter 2

Murderous Crimes and Doomed Ships

The most frightening stories about ghost ships feature glowing vessels, spooky fog, doomed crews, and fateful curses. These are the tales that are the most difficult to prove. They often have more basis in folklore and literature than in fact. Such stories are passed down over the years and accepted as truth, especially by the superstitious.

Some of the earliest tales of cursed ships go back to old Scandinavian and German legends. There is an ancient folklore tale, for example, that comes from a Norse saga about Captain Stötte, a Viking who is cursed for stealing a ring with magical powers. For his crime, the Viking gods turn him into a skeleton that does not die. Captain Stötte has to

A crew of skeletons is depicted manning a ghost ship, one of many frightening visions of legends passed along by sailors through the years.

sail a black ship for all eternity, never reaching a final resting place.

Another story originating from German legend is about Captain von Falkenberg. He is also cursed, but he tries to win back his soul by betting against the devil in a never-ending game of dice. This piece of the story about gambling with Satan was later adapted to the second *Pirates of the Caribbean* movie, *Dead Man's Chest*. In a twist in the story, Will Turner's dead father tries to gain his son's freedom from service on Davy Jones's ship, the *Flying Dutchman*, by playing dice.

Curse of the Flying Dutchman

The classic tales of ghost ships concern captains or crews who have been cursed for something they have done. The most famous of these is the tale of the Flying Dutchman. Depending on the version of the

Legend states that the ghostly captain and crew of the
Flying Dutchman are doomed to sail the sea for eternity,
cursing the fates of sailors who happen upon them.

story, the Flying Dutchman's real name is Captain Vanderdecken, or Van Straaten, or Fokke, or several other last names. He is "flying" because the captain was known for piloting his ship at swift speeds. Later versions of the tale transferred this nickname to the ship, which came to be called the *Flying Dutchman*.

According to the story, sometime during the 17th century (exact dates are not recorded), the ship encounters a terrible storm near the Cape of Good Hope off the southern tip of Africa. Captain Vanderdecken, in one version, swears to outwit God and survive the storm. In many other such tales, the captain strikes a deal with the devil to break free of the storm. There are stories, too, in which the crew and/or the captain commit a murderous crime. Whatever the case, the ship and all those on board are cursed until Judgment Day— the end of time. They are doomed to roam the seas forever on a ghost ship, never finding peace.

What is unique about the story of the *Flying Dutchman* is that anyone who sees the ship is fated to die as well. The **spectral** vessel appears to glow at night, and some say it can disguise itself by appearing to be a different ship.

Not all those who saw the *Flying Dutchman* died, however. The most famous person to say he saw the ghost ship was King George V. As a young man, sailing near the Cape of Good Hope on HMS *Bacchante* in 1881, he reported seeing "a strange red light as of a phantom ship all aglow, in the midst of which light the mast, spars and sails of a brig 200 yards . . . distant stood in strong relief."[3] A few other sailors on the *Bacchante* also said they saw the ghost ship, though what they saw, exactly, was never confirmed.

The Palatine

Many other stories about ghost ships involve murder or other crimes. One such story is about a ship called the *Palatine*. Around the year 1720, the tale goes, the *Palatine* was sailing from Holland to New England. Along the way the ship ran short of supplies, and the crew **mutinied** and killed the captain. Half the crew had died from thirst, hunger, or illness, and they took advantage of the surviving passengers by making them pay for food and water.

Glowing Ships Explained?

One proposed theory about glowing visions on Chaleur Bay was given by historian Welcome A. Greene in 1880. He believed that the glow was caused by **phosphorescent** fish called menhaden. Today many believe that Saint Elmo's fire may lead people to think they are seeing a ghost ship.

By the time the ship neared Block Island off Rhode Island, the crew had abandoned ship to escape punishment, leaving the passengers to starve. When the ship reached the shore, the situation only worsened. The people on the island plundered the ship and attacked the passengers, killing everyone but one woman who had lost her mind. They placed her on the ship, lit it on fire, and set it adrift on Chaleur Bay. Since then, the **specter** of the ship is sometimes supposedly seen, glowing from the fire, the eerie wails of the insane woman clearly heard.

The Lady Luvibund

A tale of crime also lies behind another ghost ship legend. The *Lady Luvibund* is supposedly seen along a stretch of English coastline known as the Goodwin Sands. The Goodwin Sands include about 11 miles (18km) of sandy banks in the English Channel, about 6 miles (10km) from the English mainland. Difficult to see at night and easy to run into during a storm, the Goodwin Sands have been blamed for hundreds of shipwrecks over the centuries.

It is not surprising that a ghost ship story surrounds the Goodwin Sands. According to the legend of the *Lady Luvibund*, the ship set sail from London in 1748. The ship's captain, Simon Reed, had just been married, and the ship's first mate, John Rivers, had been Reed's best man at the wedding. Rivers, however, wanted his commanding of-

Sailors spy the mysterious glow of a ghost ship. Dramatic tales of crime and passion are often a part of ghost ship legends.

ficer's bride for himself. While the captain, his bride, and the rest of the crew were belowdecks, celebrating the happy occasion, Rivers killed the ship's helmsman. He took the wheel and steered the ship into the Goodwins, where it crashed and

Newspaper Fiction

A big problem with the *Lady Luvibund* story is that no written reference about the ghost ship has been found before a February 15, 1924, article written anonymously in the *Daily Chronicle* newspaper. Some speculate that the story was invented by the newspaper to boost tourism on the English coast.

sank. Everyone on board, including the murderous Rivers, drowned.

Fifty years after the *Lady Luvibund* sank, the ghostly ship was sighted by James Westlake, captain of the *Edenbridge*. The captain reported seeing the ship headed for the Goodwins, and the sound of laughter from the honeymooners' celebration could be clearly heard. Next, around 1848, the doomed ship was supposedly spotted by an American vessel. This pattern of sightings has continued every 50 years or so, though some reports were made that did not coincide with this anniversary date.

Curse of an Indian Princess

In a ghost story originating from New Brunswick, Canada, an Indian princess is kidnapped by a pirate ship, but she gets her revenge by placing a curse on everyone on board. Doomed, as in similar ghost ship tales, to wander the seas forever, the glowing ship has been spotted off the New Brunswick coast on a number of occasions. The first reports date back as far as 1875, according to book author Dorothy Dearborn. Dearborn related that, just before seeing the glowing ghost ship, people witnessed a firestorm.

Another tale about the New Brunswick ship includes vast amounts of wealth, which may be why there is also a pirate version of the story. In this version a **schooner** with rich passengers was lost at sea. The ship was carrying everything from fine, expensive wines to gold and silver. "It is said that forty-three people drowned in the catastrophe and that when the body of one of the passengers washed up onshore a thousand pounds of bank notes were found on her body,"[4] according to Dearborn.

Chapter 3

Phantom Ships

Not all ghost ship stories begin with curses, murders, or other crimes. The majority, in fact, simply involve mysterious disappearances of sailing vessels that are later seen again, often by witnesses who did not know at the time that the ships had met disaster earlier. These are not tales of horror about sailors or ship passengers who are doomed because of some wicked deed. Instead, they are eerie sightings of unfortunate victims of the sea, who, for no known reason, appear to linger in spirit.

Sometimes these vessels are seen through banks of fog, and sometimes radio signals are received. There have also been reports by people who had

Sailors encounter an abandoned ghost ship while at the helm of their fishing vessel. Many ghost ship legends stem from stories of fateful storms and other misfortunes on the seas.

visions or **premonitions** about ships as if they had received a message from beyond a watery grave.

HMS *Eurydice*

One of the most bizarre cases concerns HMS *Eurydice*. Manned by a young crew undergoing training with the British navy, the wooden-hulled warship set sail from the West Indies in March 1878, heading for England. It had reached the English Channel when a late winter storm hit so suddenly that the crew had little time to react. The fierce winds and waves pushed the ship over onto its starboard side. Tragically, the **gunports** had been left open because the captain was planning to fire off a cannon salute upon reaching the city of Portsmouth. Saltwater flooded into the hull, and the ship quickly sank. Those who did not drown belowdecks and managed to jump into the sea quickly died of exposure in the icy waters.

Two years later a ship resembling the *Eurydice* was spotted by fishers near Sandown Bay, and similar sightings were reported over the years. The most convincing, according to author Angus Konstam, involved a submarine commander named Lipscombe. He was aboard HMS *Proteus* in 1934 when he apparently saw the *Eurydice*. "He was close to Dunnose Point when a sailing [warship] appeared as if from nowhere," reported Konstam, "and almost collided with his submarine. Lipscombe was a highly reputable witness, and he claims he was unaware of the *Eurydice* story until he heard it later while visiting the Isle of Wight. No logical explanation of his sighting can be found."[5]

The sighting was never adequately explained.

Alarming Stories

There are interesting stories related to the tragedy of the *Eurydice* involving premonitions of the disaster. According to Konstam, on March 22, the day the ship sank, a woman from Portsmouth, England, named Eleanor Becket suddenly was shaken with fear and panic. She thought she heard footsteps, too, outside her door, but no one was there. These sensations occurred around 3:50 P.M., the same time her brother drowned while on the *Eurydice*.

Around the same time, an elderly former soldier named Sir John MacNeill was dining with the Bishop of Ripon when he had a vision of a warship, its gunports open, suddenly hit by a storm. The bishop later reported that MacNeill had shouted, "Good Heavens! Why don't they close the port-holes and reef the sails?"[6]

Omens have been connected to other ghost ships, too. In a more recent case, for example, an amateur artist named Philip Jenkins painted a depiction of the submarine USS *Thresher* in 1962. He enjoyed painting submarines, though he had never been a sailor in one. Before he could give his artwork to the *Thresher* crew, however, a friend of his

The USS *Thresher* sank in the Atlantic during a diving test in April 1963, a fate that may have been foreseen by an artist who made a painting of the boat the year before.

who knew about submarines pointed out that Jenkins had painted the *Thresher* as if it were in an uncontrolled dive that would lead to disaster. In April 1963 the *Thresher* imploded while sinking to the bottom of the sea.

The *Bannockburn*, the Flying Dutchman of the Great Lakes

Possibly the most famous ghost ship of Great Lakes **nautical history** is the *Bannockburn*. This ship was a steel-hulled steam-powered vessel that was 245 feet (75m) long. It was carrying 85,000 bushels of Canadian wheat across Lake Superior in November 1902 when it disappeared without a trace. Just hours before it vanished, several witnesses on other ships and boats saw the *Bannockburn* sailing by at a good speed. All seemed well when Captain James McMaugh of the *Algonquin* spotted the ship on November 21, but later that night there was a strong storm on the lake.

Several reports the next day declared that the *Bannockburn* had been seen off the coast of Slate Island. Another report, from the *Fort William Times Journal*, said it was seen near Michipicoten Island. And a newspaper story from the *Kingston (Ont.) Daily Whig* told readers the ship had run aground on that island, but the crew was safe. The crew of the tugboat *Boynton* searched for the lost ship, guessing that perhaps it was Caribou Island, about 22 miles (35km) from Michipicoten Island, where the *Bannockburn* had run aground.

None of these sightings could be confirmed. When no one from the *Bannockburn* itself contacted any port, the ship *Favorite* was sent to find the vessel. But the *Bannockburn* was nowhere to be seen, although a single oar and life preserver were fished out of the lake. Speculations about the ship ranged from grounding against a reef to a boiler explosion to an overloaded cargo that might have caused the ship to take on water during the storm, but none were confirmed.

Since its disappearance, as author Dwight Boyer writes, numerous sailors have said they have seen "a mysterious phantom ship, most frequently sighted during the night watches as she beats to windward

Faulty Construction?

Many ship mysteries could have ordinary explanations. Lack of evidence can sometimes lead to wild speculations about disappearances. One theory about the *Bannockburn* is that a hull panel collapsed suddenly, causing the engines to drop right through into the lake, which would have caused the ship to sink very quickly.

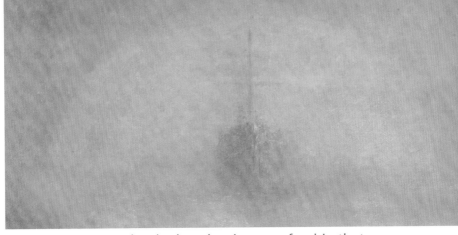

A misty vision may be the last that is seen of a ship that mysteriously disappears during its voyage, leaving others to speculate about its fate.

on her endless voyage. On stormy nights, several sailors claimed to have seen the *Bannockburn*, buffeting her way down Lake Superior, her lamps blinking in the storm scud, while in the darkened pilothouse her master looked vainly for the welcoming flash of Caribou Island Light."[7]

The København

One of the most convincing stories of ghost ships began around 1930. A Danish ship called the *København* was sailing off Cape Horn, at the southern tip of South America, in 1928. By this time in history, sailing vessels like the *København* were rarely seen anymore. Ships powered by steam or petroleum fuels were much more common. What made the Danish ship even more unusual was that it had five masts. It was the only sailing vessel on the oceans then with that many masts.

The appearance of the *København* is important because it was unmistakable, even to someone unfamiliar with ships. The ship was sailing from Argentina with a crew of 50 on December 14, 1928, when it disappeared without a trace. The reasons for her sinking could include hitting an iceberg or being hit by one of the sudden storms common in that part of the world, where winds from the Antarctic and the southern plains of Argentina meet.

Beginning in 1930, two years later, sailors began reporting seeing the *København*. They described a sailing ship with five masts just like the ill-fated ship. The accounts of the ship seemed so accurate that they are among the most reliable reports of, possibly, an actual ghost ship. There were three such sightings of the *København* that year, and then no more after that.

However, there is one explanation for these strange reappearances. When spotted, the *København* apparently had no one aboard her. One possibility is that this was not a ghost ship, but an actual abandoned ship. The captain may have ordered the crew to take to the lifeboats if his ship were sinking, but because of the storm the sailors did not survive. Ironically, the ship remained afloat, possibly for as long as two years before finally sinking as well. The crew, on the other hand, was never seen again.

Chapter 4
Mysteriously Abandoned Ships

How true the stories of many ghost ships are is very hard to determine. Like other types of ghost stories, they probably originate in folklore, literature, or from superstitious people who see shadows in the fog and think they are lost ships.

The problem with these stories is that there is no physical evidence, only eyewitness reports. But what if physical evidence *were* found? There have been many cases in which ships have been discovered floating adrift, their crews and passengers gone for no known reason. These ships have become "ghost ships" of a very real sort.

The Bermuda Triangle

The famous Bermuda Triangle is a region of the Atlantic Ocean that is famous for ship and airplane disappearances. Reaching from the island of Bermuda, down to Puerto Rico, and then northwest to the Bahamas and southern tip of Florida, the Bermuda Triangle is a stormy area that is also known for dangerous **waterspouts**, electric storms, and strange magnetic and atmospheric disturbances. Typical cases of ships lost in this area involve the vessels disappearing forever with no explanation found.

Sometimes, though, ships have been discovered emerging from the Bermuda Triangle with no one aboard them. One of the most famous stories of

The Skeptics Speak

There have been many books written about the Bermuda Triangle, but many scientists today feel that the oceans within the triangle are no more dangerous than anywhere else. These skeptics say there may be more sea accidents in the triangle merely because there is more ship and airplane traffic there.

The Bermuda Triangle is an area of the Atlantic Ocean where many ships and airplanes have mysteriously disappeared.

such a mystery involves a large sailing ship called the *Carroll A. Deering*.

The Carroll A. Deering

The *Carroll A. Deering* was discovered on January 31, 1921, at Diamond Shoals near Cape Hatteras, North Carolina, where it had run aground. No crew members were found, and they had apparently taken all their possessions with them. Navigating instruments and the captain's **log** were also gone. Red lights, a signal used in emergencies, had been run up the mast. Also confusing was the fact that meals were apparently being prepared at the time the crew abandoned ship.

The FBI launched an investigation. A number of theories were eventually eliminated, including a storm, piracy, and Russian ships trying to steal cargo because of an embargo imposed on their country.

One by one, these possibilities were eliminated, until one conclusion remained: mutiny. It was believed that either the first mate, Charles B. McClellan, or possibly the engineer, Herbert Bates, had killed Captain Willis B. Wormell for unknown reasons. The rest of the crew were either accomplices or simply did not report the murder because they did not wish to get into trouble with the authorities. They abandoned ship and tried to sink the vessel by steering toward land, but they were not successful in destroying the ship.

The remnants of the *Carroll A. Deering* sit on a beach in the Outer Banks of North Carolina, where it ran aground with its crew and key equipment mysteriously missing in January 1921.

The FBI spent several years trying to trace the crew, whom they suspected would try to find work under assumed names. After several promising leads, none of the former crew of the *Carroll A. Deering* were ever located. Just exactly what happened on this ship in January 1921 has never been fully explained.

Abandoned and Adrift

Another peculiar tale is that of the *Joyita*. A wooden yacht with a colorful history, it was once owned by a Hollywood movie director, a California businessman, the U.S. Navy, and a fishing company. It eventually ended up in the hands of Thomas "Dusty" Miller, a former officer of the British navy. He was down on his luck when he was offered a chance to start a boat service connecting Western Samoa to the Tokelau Islands in the South Pacific.

Captain Miller was anxious to set sail so that his business would profit again. He decided to leave port with one engine not working. The *Joyita* was loaded with cargo, thousands of gallons of diesel fuel, food, water, and passengers and crew totaling 25 people. It left the port in Samoa on October 3, 1955, and vanished several days later. On November 10, the ship was discovered, partially flooded with water and abandoned in the middle of the ocean, the lifeboats taken.

Because the *Joyita* had a hull made of cork, it was virtually unsinkable. Rescuers discovered plenty of food and water on board. Why, then, was it abandoned? The ship had apparently suffered some damage from a storm, but the passengers would have been safer and would have been more likely to be saved if they had stayed on board.

Some bloodied bandages were discovered (a doctor and pharmacist had been on board and apparently tried to help someone). Mattresses had been piled on top of an engine in an attempt to smother a fire, it seemed, and water was leaking into the **bilges**. The radio had been set on a distress signal that was not transmitted because of a broken antenna.

Many theories were proposed, including pirates or other criminals. Much of the cargo and money on board was missing, and there would not have been enough room on the rafts for both the cargo and people, so someone else must have taken them. Could Captain Miller have been hurt or killed by pirates?

Perhaps the ship was simply hit by a sudden storm. If the captain were unconscious or dead as a result, the crew and passengers might not have known the ship was not likely to sink and abandoned it. An investigation determined only that the ship had obviously been unsafe and, for whatever reason, abandoned. The ultimate fate of all aboard the *Joyita*, however, remains a mystery to this day.

The Mary Celeste

Some people called the mystery of the *Joyita* a modern version of the best-known deserted-ship mystery of all time: the *Mary Celeste*. This particular tale was made famous by Sir Arthur Conan Doyle, the author most renowned for his Sherlock Holmes mysteries.

The *Mary Celeste* left New York City on November 7, 1872, with ten crew members and two passengers: the captain's wife and two-year-old daughter. The *Mary Celeste* was a 103-foot-long (31m) wooden schooner about ten years old. The ship's planned destination was Gibraltar, Spain. However, something happened somewhere near a group of islands in the North Atlantic called the Azores, around November 25. That date marks the last log entry made by Captain Benjamin Briggs. The ship was found adrift, about 500 miles (805km) from the coast of Spain, by the crew of the *Dei Gratia* on December 5. The lifeboats were

Sailors from the *Dei Gratia* row out to meet the *Mary Celeste*, which was discovered abandoned and drifting off the coast of Spain in December 1872.

gone, and the people had obviously left, even
though the ship was still seaworthy.

In Doyle's short-story account, published in
1884 as "The Captain of the Polestar," when the
Dei Gratia crew boarded the *Mary Celeste* there
was a lot of evidence that people had fled the ship
quickly. Meals were on the tables, half eaten, and
more food was left cooking on a stove top.

While this part of the story was fictional, there
was real evidence left behind, too. Most disturbing
was the blood found staining three railings on the
ship. It was strange, too, that although the ship had
some water in it, there was no danger of it sinking.
The water had apparently entered the vessel during
a storm, and any experienced sailor would know it
was not going to sink.

A Possible Explanation

The mystery of the *Mary Celeste* lingered for over a century. There were many theories about the strange disappearance of all aboard. Besides piracy, there were theories of storms, waterspouts, or even **seaquakes** causing the people to flee. More bizarre ideas included UFO abduction and the effects of the Bermuda Triangle, which is actually located far from where the *Mary Celeste* was sailing.

One of the most likely explanations was put forth in a 2004 book by Brian Hicks called *The Mysterious True Story of the* Mary Celeste *and Her Missing Crew*. The author proposed the theory that

The fates of those aboard the *Mary Celeste*, depicted here in a wood engraving, remain unknown, making for one of the most famous mysteries of the sea.

Searching for Ships

Today's technology, including deep–sea-diving submarines, some of them robotic, allows more thorough exploration of the ocean floor. Perhaps in the future one of these submarines will come across a ship like the *København* or the *Bannockburn* and their mysteries will be solved.

Scientists now use remote-controlled robotic devices and other high-tech equipment to explore the ocean floor for shipwrecks.

the *Mary Celeste* was carrying industrial-grade alcohol in its cargo barrels. When the ship was found, some of the barrels were empty. It could be that someone on the ship saw that the alcohol had evaporated, which was a very dangerous situation. The alcohol could easily have sickened the crew or caught fire.

Captain Briggs, Hicks theorizes, may have told everyone to get onto the lifeboats while the ship aired out. The intention was then to reboard the ship, which explains why everyone's possessions remained on board. They tied the rafts to the **peak halyard**. Hicks points out that the peak halyard was later discovered broken. Perhaps the rafts broke free, and the captain, his family, and crew drifted helplessly away from the *Mary Celeste*.

The world's oceans are a vast expanse of waters that are still not completely understood. Although investigators might eventually discover what happened to ships that have disappeared—or at least come up with reasonable explanations—there are still mysteries that will likely continue to be passed down through the generations as legends and folklore.

Notes

Chapter One: Hazy Origins of the Ghost Ship

1. K.X. Li and Zhang Shiping, "Maritime Professional Safety: Prevention and Legislation on Personal Injuries On Board Ships." www.mersante. com/maritime_professional_safety.htm.
2. Cindy Vallar, "Superstitions and the Sea." www. cindyvallar.com/superstitions.html.

Chapter Two: Murderous Crimes and Doomed Ships

3. Quoted in Angus Konstam, *Ghost Ships: Tales of Abandoned, Doomed, and Haunted Vessels.* Guilford, CT: Lyons, 2005, p. 63.
4. Dorothy Dearborn, *New Brunswick Sea Stories: Phantom Ships and Pirate's Gold, Shipwrecks and Iron Men.* Saint John, New Brunswick, Canada: Neptune, 1998, p. 21.

Chapter Three: Phantom Ships

5. Konstam, *Ghost Ships,* p. 68.
6. Quoted in Konstam, *Ghost Ships,* p. 68.
7. Dwight Boyer, *Ghost Ships of the Great Lakes.* Cleveland: Freshwater, 1968, p. 26.

Glossary

bilges: The areas between the outer hull and the interior floors of a ship where water seepage collects.

folklore: Traditional stories, usually related as oral tales or in song, that are passed down from generation to generation.

gunports: Windows with hatch covers on the side of a battleship through which a cannon or other gun can be placed.

hull: The exterior wall of a boat or ship.

legends: Accounts of a supposedly historical event that cannot be confirmed but that may have a basis in actual events.

log: A record of daily events kept by a ship's captain.

masts: Long pieces of round wood used to support sails on a sailing ship.

mutiny: A rebellion of a ship's crew against the captain.

myths: Invented stories with no basis in fact that are passed through the generations as oral or written history.

nautical history: Historical accounts concerning ships, sailors, navigation, and shipping.

omens: Occurrences that seem to foretell a future event.

peak halyard: A line or rope attached to a pole that is attached to a mast. Pulling on the peak halyard raises it.

phenomena: Visible appearances of something.

phosphorescent: Glowing without heat, or with minimal heat, as might be seen in the case of radiation, or with some types of animals that can emit light.

premonition: A strong feeling that something, often bad, is going to happen.

Saint Elmo's fire: An electrical discharge seen most clearly off pointed objects, such as the masts of a ship. This phenomenon is named after Saint Erasmus of Formiae, the patron saint of sailors, who was also known as Saint Elmo.

schooner: A ship with at least two masts to which sails are attached.

seaquakes: Earthquakes below the ocean that can create dangerous waves on the sea's surface.

shoals: Shallow places, such as sandbars, in an ocean, lake, or river, especially in areas that are above water during low tide or when the water is otherwise low.

specter: A ghost.

spectral: Ghostly.

superstitions: Irrational beliefs, often based on a fear of the unknown.

vessel: A ship.

waterspouts: Tornado-like occurrences in the ocean, where a tubular mass of rain or swirling water forms.

yacht: A sailboat or motorboat used primarily for pleasure sailing.

For Further Exploration

Book

Angus Konstam, *Ghost Ships: Tales of Abandoned, Doomed, and Haunted Vessels.* Guildford, CT: Lyons Press, 2005. This book discusses not only ghost ships but also a variety of incidents involving spirits seen on ships and mysterious disappearances of ships.

Web Sites

Gettysburg Ghosts (www.gettysburgghosts.net/ghostships.htm). A Web site about investigating ghosts, includes stories about the *Mary Celeste, Flying Dutchman, Queen Mary*, and others.

Ghost Ships, Angels & Ghosts (www.angelsghosts. com/ghost_ships.html). Stories about ghosts and angels, information on ghost hunting, tours, and merchandise. There is a section devoted to ghost ships.

Unexplained Stuff (www.unexplainedstuff.com/ Ghosts-and-Phantoms/Ghost-Ships.html). A comprehensive encyclopedia of paranormal, magic, and religious phenomena, including a page about ghost ships.

The Un-Museum (www.unmuseum.org/phantom ship.htm). Covering topics such as UFOs and phantom ships, this site also includes a reading room for children and out-of-the-ordinary science news.

Index

Picture Credits

About the Author

Kevin Hile is a writer, editor, and Web site designer based in Michigan. A graduate of Adrian College, where he met his wife, Janet, he has been a reference book editor for almost twenty years. Hile is a former Detroit Zoo volunteer who is currently a docent and Web site manager for the Potter Park Zoo in Lansing. Deeply concerned about the environment, animals, and wildlife conservation, he is also the author of *Animal Rights* and *Little Zoo by the Red Cedar*. Hile is a regular contributor to Gale's *Contemporary Authors* series. He is also the author of *Dams and Levees* and *Centaurs* for KidHaven Press.